Preface
Metamorphoses

Steve Rushton

erbacce-press
Liverpool UK

© copyright (2022) of the poems remains with the author; Steve Rushton

All rights reserved; no part of this publication may be reproduced
in any way without the written consent of erbacce-press
5 Farrell Close, Melling, Liverpool, L31 1BU, UK

Cover-design and layout; © copyright (2022) Pascale Gouverneur
Cover images and all images herein; © copyright (2022) Steve Rushton
Editing, text layout and typesetting; © copyright (2022) Dr. Alan Corkish

erbacce-press publications Liverpool UK 2022

erbacce-press.com
ISBN: 978-1-912455-34-8

Notes

We once were two
but now are ten
with illustrations.

The original draft totalled 80 poems in two sections. This revision, nodding to Ovid's great poem about transformation and done in a mad few months, totals 300 poems in 10 sections. And roughly half aren't typically poems at all but more prose or fragments of sentences. And given that poems are all in strict meter with trochaic lines indented while prose flows intuitively and fragments are a mixture of both, formatting was problematic to say the least, especially with illustrations added. But thanks to the brilliant work of Dr Alan Corkish at erbacce-press we have a happy marriage, between layout aesthetics and the 300 entries that, whatever their merits, are at least hung perfectly.

Many thanks also to Dr Andrew Taylor, Pascale Gouverneur and all at erbacce-press; Carolyn King; Halina Rarot; Anna Maria Mickiewicz and all at Literary Waves Publishing; Professor Pete Smith; Chris Tanasescu (MARGENTO); Felix Nicholau; Nate Najar; Bob White; Lorrain Baggaley and The Youth Club.

Illustrations are based on paintings by the author.
1001. Front cover *Landslip* 25cm x 25cm oil on canvas
1002. p.9. *Slogan* 28cm x 32.5cm oil on wood (detail)
1003. p.21. *Trace* 25.5cm x 25.5cm oil on wood (detail)
1004. p.29. *Track* 25cm x 25cm oil on wood (detail)
1005. p.41. *Evidence* 25.5cm x 26cm oil on wood (detail)
1006. p.53. *Bellevue* 20cm x 20 cm oil on canvas (detail)
1007. p.71. *Battle* 22cm x 33cm oil on wood (detail)
1008. p.89. *Battle* 22cm x 33cm oil on wood (detail)
1009. p.99. *Gesture* 25cm x 25cm oil on wood (detail)
1010. p.111. *Afternoon Storm* 19cm x 32cm oil on wood (detail)
1011. p.121. *Yachts* 25cm x 25cm oil on wood (detail)
1012. Back cover *Bellevue* 20cm x 20cm oil on canvas

Sections can be read as poems, walked as walks
with meter as the pace, the scenes continuous
or not dependent on the nature of the walk
and often interrupted by a random turn
that only later fits the rambling narrative
(a fragment or a name suggesting other walks).

A stretch of road with traffic interrupting thought
is followed by an alleyway of unexpected variants
but still the pace is kept until it turns to prose.
(This richness of structural complexity
more intuitive, not filtered by overarching
methodology – refreshing yet confusing
stepping into idiosyncratic speech with its
rhythms, tones and pauses, awkward spaces.)

   When the prose returns to verse
and verse in turn returns to prose
and back and forth is there a metamorphosis with pace-embraced
vernacular and speech-enlivened
   meter or no change at all,
the two enraptured by themselves,
oblivious to influence?

   Numbers are there as a guide and are not
to be read as an integral part of the poems.

"Of bodies chang'd to various forms, I sing:"

Ovid *Metamorphoses* translated by John Dryden
(Book One, line 1)

Sections

	Pages
1-30. Preface Introduction	10
101-130. Preface Preface	22
201-230. Preface Particles	30
301-330. Preface Can I say?	42
401-430. Preface Manifesto	54
501-530. Alternative Preface for *Alter Ego*	72
601-630. Preface Epilogue	90
701-730. Preface Postscript	100
801-830. Preface Afterword	112
901-930. Preface Appendix	122
1001-1012. Preface Illustrations	
1001.	front cover
1002.	9
1003.	21
1004.	29
1005.	41
1006.	53
1007.	71
1008.	89
1009.	99
1010.	111
1011.	121
1012.	back cover
About the author	132

ILLUSTRATION 1002

1-30. Preface Introduction. The quotes in *5,6 &7* are from Restoration poet/playwright John Dryden, famous for his *Prefaces* and *Prologues*. *5* is from "An Account of the Ensuing Poem [*Annus Mirabilis*]", *6* from the Epilogue To *The Wild Gallant* When Revived in 1667 (with minor contemporary alterations), *7* from the Prologue to *All for Love, or the World Well Lost*, 1678. The quote in *25* is from the "Dryden" translation of Ovid's *Metamorphoses – Baucis and Philomin, Book 8,* Samuel Croxall. And finally, clave is written clavé throughout this collection.

1.
Of many forms becoming poems,
  poems changed to many forms
I sing (or only think I do,
encouraged by an avant-garde
aesthetic that can only write
in opposition, allied to
a contrary mentality
that sees a life antagonistic).

2.
   Lobby, Lower Ground Floor, Upper
   Basement, Basement, Lower Basement,
   Various Locations – this
collection is an Underground
Department Store. The lifts are ancient,
   escalators broken down.
A vacant store assistant stares
at changing rooms that no-one uses,
   useless things that no-one needs.

3.
Preface was the better word
(the rhythm and the rhyme of it)
yet both were common introductions –
   Prologues joked in verse attacking
   critics while the *Prefaces*
addressed a more discerning reader
   (patrons, kings and queens and lords
and ladies) lacking verse and humour.
   Both are married here – the *Prologue/*
   Preface intertwined in prose
and verse with wit and explanation,
   some would say with highfalutin
   thoughts that rise above their station
   (others shrug and turn the page).

4.
The plays and verse can never match the *Prefaces* and *Prologues* introducing them (at least with Dryden).

5.
"So then, the first happiness of the Poet's Imagination is properly Invention, or finding of the thought; the second is Fancy, or the variation, deriving or moulding of that thought as the Judgment represents it proper to the subject; the third is Elocution, or the Art of clothing and adorning that thought so found and varied, in apt, significant and sounding words: The quickness of the Imagination is seen in the Invention, the fertility in the Fancy, and the accuracy in the Expression. For the two first of these, Ovid is famous amongst the poets."

6.
"Humour is that which every day we meet,
And therefore known as every public street;
In which, if ever poets go astray,
You all can point, 'twas there they lost their way."

7.
"WHAT Flocks of Critiques hover here to-day,
As Vultures wait on Armies for their Prey,
All gaping for the Carcase of a Play!"

8.
The elevator takes us down
to windowless interiors
where artificial lighting flickers.
  Foolish shoppers hover round
in thrall to "meaningful" delights –
a tortured soul, a broken heart,
a severed head, accusing finger.

9.
   Jagger's drawling vocal diction,
   Diddley's dancing clavé beat
and Ovid's words with mighty Cupid –
   poems made to syncopate
from birds and petrol tanks to cakes and orbits.

10.
   What was foreground, what was background,
   blur beyond all recognition.

11.
No-one watching save for Netflix
   millions flicking through the options.

12.
   Verse that runs through all the organs
   (not just beating, bleeding, grieving
   in the heart).

13.
Behold the crew of Dionysus
  in disguise as bar-room sots.

14.
The liberties these bastards take!

15.
A world in strict tetrameter –
dictatorships have never been
such fun (in case you're reading, Putin).

16.
  Self-determination is
a mirror for our exegesis.

17.
  Who grows restless? Let them write.
And who grows lazy? Let them fight.

18.
A fragile ego hesitates
to play with its inconstancy.

19.
Ascending stairways into heaven
 (rock bands on the intercom).

20.
No lone authorial voice passing down wisdom/
sensitivity but opinions deliberately unreliable.

21.
Subversions of the status quo
or modulations necessary
 for a perfect poetry
society to regulate its population?

22.
    Prefaces be damned for heartless verse and prose.

23.
"Those poems are no more than pious lies,
You attribute too much to verses' sway,"
You think they give us forms, they take away
informed debate, and in its place –
an overgrowth of jumbled lines
like weeds in need of cultivation
   by an overseeing hand,
no god but more an alter ego,
   complement to verses' passion,
   critical in execution.

24.
   In the car park of a Dartmoor
   pub I saw some hippies who,
refused a drink, poured sugar down
the landlord's petrol tank.

25.
An eagle or another raptor
   briefly interrupts their play –
they crowd it out before returning
   to their other entertaining.

26.
   There's a methodology of sorts.

27.
Department store be damned, this is
a *Hotel California*
from hell – the rooms are rotten verses,
  floors are sectioned, doors ajar,
the pages turn like dirty linen,
  full of restless men and women
  waiting for a decent poem.

28.
  Preface – not a foot awry,
unless of course it's awkward prose,
too close to life for art defined
by feet and meter, abstract measure.

29.
   Where's the plot? There isn't one
(they all say that) but something like
an awkwardness of verse and prose
with meter as a smoother offer.

30.
   Dryden's was a dry approach,
a sort of class divide.

ILLUSTRATION 1003

101-130. Preface Preface

101.
Preface – eleven *Prologues* escaping jails of dependency and chained together by camaraderie with illustrations (or is it illusions?) for company forging new lives for themselves – it would have been twelve but I had to stay behind to write this.

102.
  Preface as a motley crew
of rebels, would-be academics,
   loafers, gofers, lackeys, mopers,
   hangers-on and understudies,
   mothers, daughters, sons and lovers,
   poets stealing lines from others,
   artists with a manifesto
   for a metamorphosis in verse.

103.
  Preface as a marriage made in paperwork.

104.
Aesthetics, physics,
  épater la poésie,
insouciance, iconoclasm,
  suffocating background culture.

105.
  Preface as companion in constant fights against tacit acceptance.

106.
  Preface flitting from one thought to another without following through.

107.
  Preface as Einstein elevator analogy – if you aim straight and don't move you'll always miss.

108.
  Preface as Ovidian metamorphosis.

109.

Preface says Yes to The Sex Pistols – Rick Wakeman was a better musician but Johnny Rotten was an icon.

110.

Preface – Mephistopheles descending in the Underworld Department Store in search of footwear.

111.

Preface – it might be flawed but counter-arguments are boring.

112.

Preface waiting for a *Preface*.

113.
   Preface for a comedy –
the poet thinks, the critic thinks
the poet stinks. The end is not
a pretty sight – they both begin to bloody write.

114.
   Preface as a Mephistophelean
   metamorphosis from Dr Faustus
   back to fertile fields of Troy.

115.
   Preface for a tragedy.
The poets write. Their verse is trite.
They realize. The end.

116.
   Preface – no more anecdotes
that think they have a joke in them
but underneath are self-promotion.

117.
  Preface for a panoply
of characters fulfilled by verse
and none the worse for that although
the poetry's another matter.

118.
  Preface as a tendency
to minor criminality
with poetry a hapless victim –
  so they say.

119.
  Preface as a double-bass,
a counterpoint to violins.

120.
  Preface as a pressing matter.

121.

Preface – forging upwards like plant growth with oxygen a by-product of creation.

122.

Preface rising against empires of books with nothing to lose but back covers.

123.

Preface as abstract painting throwing off shackles of confining figuration.

124.

Preface as colour as colour and not the colour of something.

125.

Preface as mould surrounding decaying matter – the only new growth.

126.

Preface approaching apotheosis.

127.

Preface as new spring (a metaphor too far or the last breath of a dying *Preface*).

128.
Preface takes the piss (its business).

129.
Nothing ends until I say so.

130.
Carry on.

ILLUSTRATION 1004

201-230. Preface Particles

201.
When do parts or particles become a wave
and does it take a certain number or amount –
a ton of parts or particles becomes a wave,
ten thousand parts or particles become a wave
(poor Helen, knowing ships will come, she must be
                                      brave),
a frequency of parts or particles becomes
a tidal wave – identifiable as such
with common features and a build-up of momentum?

202.
"look pretty young, but I'm just back-dated, yeah."
                            The Who *Substitute* 1966

203.

The tests were made with all the parts compared/contrasted, in the combinations listed.

1, 101,	101, 201,	801, 901,
2, 102,	102, 202,	802, 902,
…	...	…
30, 130.	130, 230.	830, 930.

1001, 1,	1012, 1,
1001, 2,	1012, 2,
…	...
1001, 930.	1012, 930.

1002, 1,	1003, 101,	1011, 901,
1002, 2,	1003, 102,	1011, 902,
…	…	…
1002, 30.	1003, 130.	1011, 930.

204.
Metaphor for all this metamorphosis –
the double-slit experiment in quantum physics.

205.
Initiatives were taken in various sections to the
exclusion of all else including the specific reason
a passage was written in the first place.

206.
Metered verse's artificiality
is checked and prose is measured off
against a more restrictive other.

207.
Hanging in the air like birds
of prey in search of sustenance.

208.
A counterpoint in English breakfasts –
   crispy bacon, runny eggs.

209.
And exegesis is a platform
   for our self-determinations.

210.
   Concept album tracks instead of vinyl singles.

211.
   Semi-clumsy dancer slowly
   finds her feet amongst the dusty
   footsteps of distinguished predecessors.

212.
   In a space that's been vacated,
   in a car-park nearly full.

213.
Is this a *Preface* for a *Preface*
  for a *Preface* for a *Preface*
  for a *Preface* for a *Preface*
  for a *Preface* for a *Preface*
  for a *Preface* for a *Preface*
  for a *Preface* or a *Preface*
  for a *Preface* for a *Preface*
  for a *Preface* for a *Preface*
  for a *Preface* for a *Preface*
  for a *Preface* for a *Preface*
  for a *Preface* for a *Prologue*
or a *Preface* for a *Preface*
  for a *Preface* for a *Preface*
  for a *Preface* for a *Preface*
  for a *Preface* for a *Preface*
  for a *Preface* for a *Prologue*
  for a *Poetry Collection*
or a *Preface* for a *Preface*
  for a *Preface* for a *Preface*
  for a *Preface* for a *Preface*
  for a *Preface* for a *Preface*
  for a *Prologue* for a *Poetry Collection* for a *Preface*?

214.
    Frankenstein-like combinations,
    Igor for a muse.

215.
A dressing is depressing
   if the salad isn't fresh.

216.
More mallet than a scalpel
   but it's sculpture after all.

217.
And weaponizing – what a word!
Its current popularity
in battles for a certain party
   makes compulsive reading but
the fashion (never mind the fallout)
   happened twenty years ago.

218.
The foolish are derided by
the not so foolish and perspective
   seems to disappear inside
a fog of factional invective.

219.
   Was there right and wrong? Of course,
though where it was, because of fog,
became impossible to tell
although at first it all seemed clearer.

220.
   Chalk and cheese are both the same
(though in the name of no-one present).

221.
   Call me out as one more lazy dilettante.

222.
So now the fog has lifted and
beyond the six that lost their lives
in Washington the numbers rise
in multiples of multiples
expanding exponentially
and inexplicably if thinking
   purely in political
and relativist terms – we know
that Trump in his denial of
democracy endangered truth
but Putin in ignoring truth
denies democracy – equations
   are misleading but their lessons
   are persuading. All the talk
of NATO and expansion and
the threat to Russia's borders by
the *Morning Star* and others seems
irrelevant to genocide
or something like it practised on
the streets of Bucha – double standard
   commentators quote Mai Lai
and other western "aberrations",
   say they are the norm. But Putin's
   government is not the same,
and even if it's similar
in some respects must be resisted
   with the same degree of anger
   saved for western capital's
expansionist adventures, not
just qualified by history
and mitigating circumstance.

223.
To nullify the best attempts
and vilify the best attempters.

224.
  Can I say these parts are part
of something else, a wave perhaps?

225.
And can I say (I think I can)
with particles as poetry
and waves as prose, duality
as alternating, altercating
   alter egos, this is just
another type of double-slit experiment?

226.
"You can't judge a book by looking at the cover." Bo Diddley 1962

227.
A richness imitators rarely managed
 (with the Rolling Stones a notable exception).

228.
Osmosis on the lead guitar.

229.
And all those rock and roll bands run over
by time and insignificance – we salute you!

230.
   Preface – anti Status Quo.

ILLUSTRATION 1005

301-330. Preface Can I say?

301.
 The nature of a *Preface*, what it does
and how it's written – can an exploration
 of its character and features find
a way to reinvent the art of verse?

302.
Like players acting on a page
or fools redundant in a world
of fools where fashion matters more
than matter, less than silly money,
 more or less than flattery,
which fashion is, in worlds of inequality.

303.

"A tiger's leap into the thicket of the past."
  Walter Benjamin *On the Concept of History*
  1940 (a metered translation)

304.

And first was last (and last the first)
but seen the first if front to back.

305.

An absent sun, or one that's only seen reflected.

306.

  Minor voices shrill, the message
  bludgeoning an audience,
but can I say this still might be
the one-hit wonder that gets played
from time to time, as much for zeitgeist
  (or anticipation of)
than unrelenting yet restrained
attacks upon received convention?

307.
   Can I say historical perspective's not
a plaything to be used whenever
   lack of sense of humour beckons?

308.
   Can I say I'm playing with artistic fire
(although of matchstick-size dimensions)?

309.
Can I say that nonetheless without occasional
forays into the long grass we all get stuck in
the mud, wellington boots no protection against
passivity of ahistorical confusion?

310.
Can I say *Illustrations* are too Abstract
Expressionist for my liking, a harkening back to
some pre-post-modern time when artists foolishly
believed…in something, anything, apart from their
own sense of irony (painting) or integrity (poetry),
so different in trajectory these disciplines – if they
only met for a drink some time?

311.
And can I say the land of absurdity is littered with used food wrappers, empty beer cans and bottles of wine, and the faint aroma of over-extended egos?

312.
And can I say (referencing a phrase and film so dreadfully adapted by a media-obsessed, *experience-lite* consumer culture to be ridiculous if it wasn't so tragic) that unlike napalm the smell of over-extended egos in the morning, as long as one wasn't witness to the barrage of invective emanating from the previous night (I was in the kitchen when it happened!) can be quite pleasant, a stimulus to further activity?

313.
And can I say, by way of disclaimer, that someone has probably done this before, but not to my knowledge? (Encyclopaedic awareness of all things poetic not my specialism.)

314.
The tyranny of *me*
The tyranny of *media*
The tyranny of *mediocrity*

315.
And can I say this *Preface/Prologue's*
  positively Drydenesque,
didacticism reinvented,
  all the rest as secondary?

316.
  Can I say it's never there
until it's read (interpretations
  hover round like multiverses)?

317.
   Can I say that tempted as
I am by plans of offbeat formats,
   sections overlapping, wrapped
inside each other, intertwined
by different fonts, the whole a layout
   artist's playground, there's a problem
   relegating poetry
into a kind of category –
   Words in Need of Graphics for Support?

318.
And can we see habitual
"o woe is me" production lines
enjoying sad emojis at
the end of each emotive page?
Not likely, darling!

319.
   Can I say "away with sober
   presentations from the past,
the future's not *Helvetica*
or *Arial* but something more
experimental, *Times New Roman*
   Reinvented for example –
   Ovid plays Augustus for
the confidence of Julia
(the mother or the daughter, well,
it's difficult to tell – and all this
   in a typeface)?"

320.
"When will we realize that we can no longer write like in the '60s and '70s' and '80s?" Felix Nicholau, "The Ovidiu file reopened at the headquarters of computational prosody" (*Arca... Number 1,366,* 2022).

321.
Preface Metamorphoses –
a Mephistophelian pact
between the devil and the deep blue sea –
I'll drown for you, you burn for me.

322.
Golden memories of youth as proto-punk teenage spotty drummer rebelling against dinosaurs of prog rock. But enough of nostalgia.

323.
"This much awaited breakaway from established/ossified styles and approaches." Chris Tanasescu, aka MARGENTO, email conversation, March 2022.

324.
"When one has been exposed to the larger artistic rumble, one can afford innovating through long-forgotten recipes. These days they write like in the '60s and boast their grandeur." Felix Nicholau, email conversation, March 2022.

325.
Some may feel a lone authorial and mostly sincere voice is an ultimate bulwark against barbarism, whereas I, in thrall to traditions from Ovid to Swift, believe it's time for a shift, to a poetry of disparate voices where truth (amongst other things) is debatable.

326.
What's brought to the table – a sort of poetical, visual, musical meze without the main course to worry about.

327.
A parent hosting Sunday lunch.

328.
Or Sunday lunch?

329.
　Soliloquies occur of course
occasionally to compliment.

330.
And even lukewarm comments are a stimulus
to further action, impetus for one more thought.

ILLUSTRATION 1006

401-430. Preface Manifesto (for wit/debate in poetry – with reference to *Scandi-Noir*)

401.
I must confess a prejudice.
I'm bored by all the anecdotes
that start with lines like "I did this"
and "I did that" – I'm not the perfect
   dinner-party guest I know.
And recent stand-up comedy
along these lines I cannot stand.
And quick fire sit-com repartee –
like *Friends* and all those "housey-housey"
   shows – I hate. But give me *Scandi-
   Noir* or something with a decomposing body, someone chasing
   someone else – hilarious!

402.
"So where's the decomposing body?"
   "Over there, surrounded by
a coterie of acolytes."
"Describe them." "Well, a lack of style
is prevalent, a fashionista's
   seminar it's not, although
there are some actors practising,
but mostly people shuffle papers."
   "Age?" "It ranges from the teenage
   prodigy to those without
a proper hobby." "Suspects?" "Well,
it's all of them, though they will argue
   they've been keeping decomposing
   bodies live for quite a while."
"Do you agree?" "Well, possibly."

403.
There was a time when poetry
was full of wit and quick debate
(the language was arcane, but then
it was a half-millennium ago).

404.
It's all first person singulars!
(I love, I hate, I wander, write,
I am alone in this poetic
 state – the habit takes a form
of holding forth as yet unchallenged.)

405.
 I'm not saying there's no wit/
debate but that disparities
in favour of the monologue
opposed to witty dialogue
exist. I could be wrong I know,
it's not the point. The point is this –
to rally troops for one more crazy
 fucked-up venture. I'm recruiting –
 willing soldiers, lovers, liggers – come along.

406.
Can dialogue exist if written
 by an all-controlling hand?
The beauty of an argument
is in its crazy improvising
 unpredictability.
Can poets copy this without
resorting to an artifice,
pretending with a false conceit?
(And isn't all conceit conceit?)

407.
And customs, since beginnings of
Romanticism, find a poet
 isolated. Things were different
 once upon a time, there were
communities of poets writing,
 bouncing wit about like footballs.

408.
Got to dash – you'll never guess!
They've just discovered fifteen decomposing bodies stuck inside
a TV set, the crew and actors
   apoplectic, wanting answers –
   they should know, they play detectives
   then demand I run the show!

409.
Although it's mainly monologue
extolling use of dialogue –
the verses are to some extent
detached, and complement each other –
   nonetheless to argue that
they constitute a conversation
   stretches credibility.

410.
Concerning wit, opinion is
divided on a definition.
   Mine is this, for what it's worth –
there is debate, because of its
complexity and changing nature
   over time. Suffice to say
for now at least that wit is what
a writer/reader says, so if
you think that Wordsworth's *Daffodils*
is witty, well, it bloody is.

411.
The plots can be depressing – constant
   angst, suspicion, fear, it's like
Romanticism's found a home
in modern life, in purgatorial *IKEA*.

412.
A sense of order can be found
if someone works their fingers to the bloody bone.
It's funny, since detective fiction
   started back with *Sherlock Holmes*,
the genre has increasingly
demanded this intensity
from overworked protagonists.

413.
Without a gripe they may not want
a second pint (or third or fourth –
depressing thought for all concerned)
and stick to moderation in
their drinking habits, joining all
the part-time boozers going home
un-metamorphosised by beer
(their only fear). And what did Titian,
   famous painter, say – someone
who has a drink and not a second
   doesn't know what drinking is?

414.
Is witty funny? Well, not necessarily.
There is a sense that's what been said,
the way it's said, has not been done
so well before, or if not that,
then recently. And more than that,
there is a quick perceptiveness,
a way of seeing differently,
that makes a witty poem stand out
   from the crowd. It might be funny,
   or might not. A union
between what's said/the way it's said,
concision in one's verse and thoughts
or, contrawise, expansiveness
in mind and words or, even better,
   rhythms in the way one thinks/
the way one writes, are part of it –
but then the unexpected plays
a part as well, and more than that,
and yes I know it has been said
before but still there is a truth,
subjectively, that what one says
or thinks or sees as witty *is*.

415.
An age of wit (not ours of course)
could benefit from bold reviving,
   not one poet banging on
but many playing in a verse
accessible and witty with
a devil in the poetry.

416.
Hegemonies must be resisted.

417.
   Judgements made and any gossip
     (tittle-tattle) that's attached –
the poet's lot, a lack of wit,
the relevance of recent verses
     or, what's more, a lack of it,
the fact that modern life is missing
     from appalling advertising,
     in-between bad versifying,
     too much drinking, not enough
attention paid to those who have
a claim upon his memory
(forgetfulness is in the blood) –
he owes me dinner or some money,
     something that he told me yes-
terday while laughing wasn't funny,
     funny that he's absent when
he says all life is in the present –
     all these things that might or might not
     find a place in what he's writing
     or you're thinking, won't be what
he's thinking when he's writing or
reviewing writing. So, in short,
detaching meanings from proceedings
     he will leave to you.

418.
Forever wanting knowing poems,
   knowing always wanting poems.

419.
   Poets need to best their predecessors or go down in trying.
   Sentimental homages
will never win an audience
but battles will. So play it dirty,
   on a field that's full of ruts
and fools and wits and win with fouls
and kicks and sins, it doesn't matter –
   better than to bow and flatter.

420.

   Modest actors, writers, poets
   don't like praise or accolades –
the crowded halls and loud applause
can bore, it's just the perfect phrase
that gets them every time, although
it's sniffed at till it's recognised,
though credit's due, its frequency
is like a truffle in the woods –
too many mushrooms lie around,
inedible, or tasting awful –
   skill is needed in selection,
   otherwise, there'll be a problem
   for a gourmet's delicately
   tuned digestion.

421.

   Advocating competitions
   seemed to be the right solution.
   Who's to judge them? There's the problem –
   Ayers, McGough, McMillan, Cope
and others in the witty camp
content with how things are – the praise
of *Poetry* (won't) *Please, The Verb*
and other shows – I cannot cope.

422.
What follows on is commonplace
but vanity will make it worse.
The critics help, or try at least,
with truth and reason in consid-
eration of a poet's lot
and well applied? Well, you decide.

423.
And taking statements at the station,
  warn them one more line of verse,
I'll throw the bloody book at them.
And worse than that (what could be worse)
if they attempt to justify
their lines of shite with explanations –
  throw away the fucking key!

424.
A single voice, the perfect I,
all sensitive, intuitive,
a solitary commentator
　on our lives – Romanticism
　was and is, in spite of many
　movements since, we still have this,
the single voice, the perfect I.

I wandered lonely as a cloud,
How do I love thee? Let me count the ways.
i like my body when it is with your
I hold with those who favor fire.
I thought that love would last forever: I was wrong.
I hope to see my Pilot face to face
When I have fears that I may cease to be
Because I could not stop for Death
As I grew older
*　I lie on my back at midnight*
*　Now as I was young and easy*
*　I Know Why The Caged Bird Sings*
I am in need of music
*　Traveling through the dark I found a deer*
I saw the best minds of my generation
*　I am silver and exact. I have no preconceptions.*
*　Yes you have.*

4.24a
   Wordsworth, Browning, Cummings, Frost,
   Auden, Tennyson, Keats, Dickenson,
   Hughes, Kerouac, Thomas, Angelou,
   Bishop, Stafford, Ginsberg, Plath.

425.
Of choirs sounding all the same,
or so it seems, I sing (or only
   think I do, encouraged by
an avant-garde aesthetic that
can only write in opposition,
   allied to a contrary
mentality that sees a life
antagonistic).

426.
   Betters sneer, look down and scoff,
as this does to its lessers, those
poor poets who, in need of wit,
will say sincerity is it,
the non plus ultra of the verse,
with humour waiting in the wings,
too scared of limelight, centre stage,
while drips will pine and bleed upon
the printed page, and steal each scene,
and punters, lacking any spleen,
will substitute a grieving heart.
But wait, a poet with some guts
shouts "Drips, exeunt!" The stage is set
at last for wit. The lights go up
and ushers bustle, seats are emptied.
   Lines are read to turning backs
who lacking any kind of love
for work without a broken heart
ignore this lighter type of verse,
weighed down, of course, by something worse
than gravity, and then depart.

427.
And now's the time for something new
(but then this sentence is the oldest one I know).

428.
To find a verse that's never out
of time will take more time than time.

429.
Triumphant yet inconsequential.

430.
  Sarah Lund

ILLUSTRATION 1007

501-530. Alternative Preface for *Alter Ego*, one of five "translations" of an absent original featured in MARGENTO, Steve Rushton, Taner Murat, *Various Wanted* (Timpul 2021, also Google Books and Google Play and performed by Ovid with Reverb at Ventnor Fringe Festival and Tanglewoodstock – excerpts on YouTube).

501.
Based on an addendum to a long poem, yet in final editing becoming *Preface*, something to be read before, rather than after, the verse. And then, prior to publication, examples were sought and lines written tying ends together. And even then more seemed necessary, not as the original *Preface*, as the proof had already gone to the printers. So a plan for a stand-alone work began, a development using a format of notes familiar from previous publications.

502.
Written for conference as part of a panel entitled "Back to the Future: Metamorphoses: Poetry Trans-formed", presenting tradition as yesterday's contemporary, ripe for re-invention, re-interpretation, happening anyway, irrespective of poetic intervention and historical reconsideration, twin drivers all the more necessary as abdicating responsibility is tantamount to taking hands off the steering wheel and discarding the map or satnav.

503.
The planned journey, from great Roman poet's first collection of verse written in a distinctive anti-establishment rhythm, to Elizabethan and Restoration London's re-inventing of Ovid in an age of wit and pentameter, then on to 21st century fusions of poetry and music, ended up less an epic trek from the past and more a series of day trips.

504.
The sequence of notes – each individually planned but no further than that, the next barely a shadow on the screen while the previous was being written, all connected by a mixture of chance, intuition and after-the-fact attempts at design – feels familiar, a template for bad chess, improvised music, life, the development of language.

505.
More in tune with skipping in and out of bed than celebrating Empire, the paired couplet form encouraging an intimacy absent from constant hexameter repetitions of Roman epics redolent of marching armies and unbounded frontiers.

506.
Ironically, Christopher Marlowe, translator of Ovid's *Amores* into English rhyming iambic pentameter couplets, went on to write the most striking of military expansionist plays in *Tamburlaine the Great Part 1*.

507.
Ovid was exiled. Marlowe suffered physical dislocation (he was stabbed in the eye and his *Certaine of Ovids Elegies* burned by the Bishop of Croydon). John Dryden (another translator) suffered religious and career dislocation struggling with shifting power battles in Reformation England.

508.
Debates on rhythm, mirrored in the many voices
   (all the poet/lover's) in the verses of *Amores*.

509.
Of all the rhythms out of Sub-Saharan Africa, Bo Diddley's is closest to the original clavé beat – in fact, one of its two variations (1,4,7,11,13) is the clavé beat, the other being 1,4,7,*10*,13. Diddley played both, as did other Bo Diddley beat performers.

510.

The notation used here is from 1 to 16 rather than the usual "1e&a2e&a3e&a4e&a", making it easier to compare rhythmic patterns.

511.

The right hand plays eight beats to the bar – trochaic tetrameter –a rhythm the left hand both agrees with and argues against, as if to say "yes, but" in constant repetition.

512.

In sixteenths, the right hand of a Bo Diddley beat falls in regular order (1,3,5,7,9,11,13,15) with accents on 1,5,9 and 13 (the first, third, fifth and seventh beat). The left hand, playing a syncopation of 1,4,7,11,13, has five accented beats to the right hand's four. Of those five, two (the first and last) agree with the right hand, both falling on beats 1 and 13. The middle three skip round the middle two right-hand accented beats, the second left-hand beat arriving a sixteenth before the second accented right hand-beat. The third and fourth left-hand beats frame the third right-hand accented beat at 7,9,11.

513.
The Bossa Nova is closest to the Bo Diddley beat yet different in feel – just one sixteenth movement in the last accent metamorphosizing rhythm.

514.
The other Bo Diddley pattern mentioned earlier (1,4,7,10,13) is more dynamic, the third beat syncopated, falling in-between both accented and unaccented trochaic tetrameter beats 9 and 11. The rhythm used in *Alter Ego* (1,4,9,11,13) agrees more rather than less with the right hand, on the third, as well as the first and last beat.

515.

A	**1**	2	*3*	4	**5**	6	7	8	**9**	10	*11*	12	**13**	14	*15*	16
B	**1**	2	3	**4**	5	6	**7**	8	9	10	**11**	12	**13**	14	15	16
C	**1**	2	3	**4**	5	6	**7**	8	9	**10**	11	12	**13**	14	15	16
D	**1**	2	3	**4**	5	6	7	8	**9**	10	**11**	12	**13**	14	15	16
E	**1**	2	3	**4**	5	6	**7**	8	9	10	**11**	12	13	**14**	15	16

A – right-hand beat (accents in bold, un-accented-beats in italics)
B – left-hand beat, Bo Diddley version 1
C – left-hand beat, Bo Diddley version 2
D – left-hand beat, *Alter Ego*
E – left-hand beat, Bossa Nova

516.
"The way Rushton describes Bossa Nova isn't really Bossa Nova but it is the gringo jazz musician conception of the Bossa Nova pattern. The thing about Bossa Nova that separates it from other Latin music is that it isn't based on a strict 'clavé' or pattern; Bossa Nova is an aesthetic that is derived from Samba which has its roots in West Africa ... so they're all cousins, and Samba has a number of syncopations that weave together to create the rhythm. Bossa Nova is a distillation of Samba to its most basic and understated presentation. Rhythmically it is a great deal more nuanced and dynamic than a two measure pattern whereas much other Latin music requires the pattern to be fairly strict and the Bo Diddley thing is absolutely based on the African tradition from which they all came" Nate Najar, American guitarist, composer and producer, based in St. Petersburg, Florida. His partner, Daniela Soledade, a rising star among legends in the Brazilian music scene, heir to the throne of Bossa Nova, is highly acclaimed for her poignantly expressive vocal style and hyper-intimate aesthetic, drawing from amalgams of authentic Bossa Nova, Samba, Música popular brasileira (MPB), and American Popular Song.

517.

Rehearsals began for a performance of the poem *Alter Ego* as a fusion of Ovidian and Bo Diddley influence. Different approaches were attempted – reciting verse in one breath, using beat as background, breaking verse into couplets and triplets. Finally, a solution was found, in part borrowed from The Rolling Stones' *Not Fade Away*, where a Bo Diddley rhythm is played in 4/4 time on the drums, a riff on guitar, vocals sitting on top, spoken in and out of beat, an intuitive reading changing with each recital, an impro lead with deadpan tone on enthusiastic backing, creating contrasts of sounds, the Bo Diddley drums containing both strict four-beat and syncopated time played off against the guitar's two-bar pattern, vocals and backing vocals slipping in and out, often arguing with each other as well as with the music in extra layers of syncopation, sections played without drums, guitar making a repeating tune similar to rock and roll crooning classics such as *Teenager in Love*, providing respite from driving beat, echoing traditional sets/LPs where rockers would be followed by slow numbers. Or the guitar drops out, drums and vocals sounding more insistent and parade-ground, excerpts from classic tracks (*Not Fade Away*, *Who Do You Love?*) rubbing against translations from Ovid, creating fractured timelines (present to recent and ancient past). And all this framed by a name-checking of performers borrowing from Bo Diddley and writers adapting Ovid and this interrupted by original material with beat as subject matter in all its historical and cultural metamorphoses. And the whole an assemblage (or is it bricolage?) reminiscent (in dreams anyway) of the second-side medley from The Beatles *Abbey Road*.

518.
The subject of discussion in The Big Bopper's *Chantilly Lace* is probably not as important as the beat and vocal delivery, though there is wit in the one-sided telephone conversation, especially the repeated "buts" as our singer struggles to get a word in edgeways.

519.
Performance and lyrics are perfectly harmonized in the work of Ella Fitzgerald and Louis Armstrong – Ella's cut-glass enunciation often striking an Apollonian clear and rational tone compared to Louis' more impassioned Dionysian delivery.

520.
Ovid's original elegiac rhythm was an alternate six/five feet couplet. Using only accented beats, this can be developed with drum patterns – for example, in a triple triplet paradiddle, translating into lines such as "What do you think of my/ po - et - ry?" "Rubbish!"
     1 2 3   1 2 3   1 2 3   1 2

521.
The Ovidian and Bo Diddley beats were practised under oppressive slave regimes prohibiting free forms of expression.

522.

I wonder about mixtures of poetry and prose in this, whatever it is. Could they too be opposites, prose perhaps Dionysian excess spreading over the surface like the shadow of some predatory eagle engulfing Ganymede, pissing in the wind? Or a drunken accident, red wine spilling from an upturned bottle, flowing out and only slowing when exhausted, not knowing limits except in the natural tide of events, one wave after another, verse the white page and scribblings constrained within rectangles of form, desperately trying to imitate that which could flood it with colour and potency? Or the author, deliberately drinking too much wine, waiting for happy accidents – to be captured and labelled prose poetry or, in analytical mode, dissected and ordered in line lengths like a coke-sniffing aficionado craving a buzz?

523.
A Nebbiolo to poetry's Barolo, perfectly
suitable for everyday activity but lacking
that special-occasion something.

524.
Is verse an over-baked dessert
(desserts are stressed the wrong way round),
a cake that's best in nascent form?

525.
"The poet constructs his own importance, apart from the established hierarchies."

John Huntington, *Ambition, Rank, and Poetry in 1590s England*, University of Illinois Press, 2001.

Huntington's book explores 1590s England and its poetry scene, identifying certain non-aristocratic writers who try, by verse, to set up an alternative culture, a poetocracy where knowledge and expression challenges "established hierarchies". The phrase *cultural capital* appears, as if the poet were some Renaissance broker selling futures. And with it, obscurity, in part to protect writers but also to exact effort from readers, who must be up to scratch in this new order. Dunces of the aristocracy fail, as do the *hoi polloi* – no multi-layered approach with something-for-everyone here, more aspirational meritocracy. Parallels throughout cultural history abound, including understandable obscurantism in post-war Eastern Europe. But more than that, Reformation English poetry is presaged, with its elites and learned verse.

526.
20th century subcultural styles arrived at the pantheon
quicker than Huntington's poets, though things
were moving faster by then, the Mohican switch
from rebellious icon to London postcard spectacular
in speed, a mix of capital's voracious appetite for
assimilation and punk's ability to shed skins as it
went through various new waves.

527.
If all is conscious conversation it's debate,
if all insentient, a dream,
all accidental, more a drunken ramble
   (in-between the verses).

528.
Based on a variation of the Bo Diddley beat, done instinctively (I'm a drummer, so probably that's why), but after the fact I found parallels between histories of the Bo Diddley rhythm and Ovid. And in writing a *Preface* for *Various Wanted*, the book containing *Alter Ego*, along with other translations of *Thanks to Ovid*, and in conversation with MARGENTO, who is also a rock and roll aficionado, though we have musical differences of taste, which is great, I wrote the *Preface* with a feel of an old LP back cover, with gushing text emulating the flavour of vinyl inside, and performance bringing disparate elements together – Ovid in translation next to *Not Fade Away* and *Who Do You Love?*, and Bo Diddley beats for *Amores*, and culture spanning centuries mixed in a thirty-minute bash, and this, whatever it is, perhaps unconsciously adopting the structure of a poetry collection where elements riff round a central theme, some independently as things in themselves, others semi-autonomous, needing context for meaning.

529.
"In simplest terms, MARGENTO is the Romanian poet and translator Chris Tanasescu. At the same time, MARGENTO could be described as a rock band, a multimedia performance troupe, and an international coalition of writers and translators." Martin Woodside, review of MARGENTO *Nomadosofia/ Nomadosophy* (Editura Max Blecher, 2012).

530.
Strict rhythm allows a reader unfamiliar with text (but familiar with rules of regular meter) to engage with verse, important for a poet relying on constant beat in page poetry. The trick of course is to avoid monotony.

ILLUSTRATION 1008

601-630. Preface Epilogue. Quotes in *601* and *615* are from the "Dryden" *Metamorphoses* – *601* from *The Passion of Biblis* (Book 9, John Gay and Alexander Pope), *615* from *The Story of Ceyx and Alcyone* (Book 11, Samuel Croxall)

601.
"The pencil then in her fair hand she held,
By fear discouraged, but by love compelled.
She writes, then blots, writes on, then blots again,
Likes it as fit, then razes it as vain:"

602.
The wine, the soup, the conversations,
   screaming kids, a friend invited
      feeling awkward, silences.

603.
La Nouvelle Vague, *À bout de souffle*,
　Jeanne Moreau, Jean-Paul Belmondo,
　Alphaville.

604.
From Ancient Greece and Rome
to Reformation London
　and the present day.

605.
Like crazy rubber balls that bounce
beyond a poet's poor control.

606.
A literary *digestif*?

607.
They know not what they do, the fools,
believing truth when other forces shape the world.

608.
Sigourney Weaver

609.
　Cyclops incognito not
despite my verse myopia.

610.
And all the voices turned to one
with drums and dawn approaching.

611.
Ovid of course in Tomis I return again.
The sounds of war – once more the city
　is a borderland between the Western
　European and the Asian hinterlands.

612.
　Ovid amongst the Scythians by Delacroix –
the poet sits surrounded by the rolling hills,
surrounded by a nothingness,
the local population are ambivalent.

613.
　Fighting relegation, three games to go
　and a poor goal difference.

614.
Revised and expanded, the two original sections still at the centre but framed in a tribute to Ovid's *Metamorphoses* with the same theme but a new title, a homage to days of pre-poem prose poems and *Prologues*.

615.
"Down with the vessel sink into the main
The many, never more to rise again.
Some few on scattered planks, with fruitless care,
Lay hold and swim; but while they swim, despair."

616.
Without the numbers what was needed.

617.
   Undercurrent, undertow,
I see the waves then hear their alter
   egos pulling shingle back into the sea –
repeat, repeat.

618.
And so the drums monotonous
replace a syncopated beat
or try their best. A Troy defeated,
   Menelaus, Helen sacked,
a marriage made of myth in tatters.

619.
   Wit in thrall to feet and meter
   falling for an ancient writer,
   writing more and, in the process,
   falling further.

620.
   Altercations, alterations
   conversations, replications,
   variations minimal
but infinite (inside a head).

621.
A hundred years of mediocre.

622.
   Tories wrote in verse while Whigs
were novel-loving scribes – discuss!

623.
The theme of change infecting sections
   in a constant back and forth.

624.
Conservative or radical,
an undertow or undercurrent?

625.
Eighty poems in two parts expanding into this self-promoting, self-mocking poetry-mocking mini-mock-epic, a mix that doesn't know its place or if it does forgets immediately.

626.
To drown in useless indecision.

627.
   Gravitas as rhetoric
and realigned and reassigned
as necessary.

628.
"Express elevator to hell – going down!"
   (*Aliens* James Cameron 1986)

629.
An absent *If,*
a Lindsay Anderson-less place
of public schools controlling all
and sundry other institutions
   on their deathbeds.

630.
   Poems read without the numbers –
   subjects blending into one
like conversations overheard at parties.

ILLUSTRATION 1009

701-730. Preface Postscript. Quotes from *Literary Pictures of Kyiv* by Halina Rarot, translated by Anna Maria Mickiewicz, Stan Mickiewicz and Steve Rushton. Published by Literary Waves 2022.

701.
"Let silence then ring! Let great souls bear the suffering of Kyiv in silence. And let a bright thread of hope shine through this black silence, more and more visible to us every day."

702.
"The spirit of place, like a great grey bird, carefully guards its spaces, able to expand only due to acquired, nostalgic longing. From Lipki, along the Dnieper hill, there are thoughtful parks filled with the sun, the brilliance of water and the changing sapphire of Kyiv; they reveal themselves, so as not to disappear. Around the next bend there are secluded dating sites, in the green of chestnut trees and acacia everything becomes brighter and, in the end, we are completely enveloped in the sparkling, unreal beauty of palaces, churches, a space imbued with concrete and painfully delightful details of the riverside oikumene."

703.
"The modern heart of the Kyiv metropolis is the metro, a unique communication artery living its life and at the same time subordinating the entire city to itself, transporting one million seven hundred thousand people a day, making them dependent on each other, determining the value of the apartment, the meeting place, the choice of book to read, the manner of suicide or the time of the last kiss."

704.
"There is a most visible flawed utopianism in Kyivian philosophy, an inevitable disappointment, crying with regret 'why am I late?'"

705.
"Longing, although it is one of the components of love, is a wider feeling than love (you can miss what you have not seen or had)."

706.
Expanding fields of nothing changing.
　Shadows sinking in the mud.
A sense of time defaulting (peace
in pieces always was its battered
　state). Apart but also part,
a part but also not. More palette
　than an orbit. Art a measure
　of immortals. Battlefields
with dying waiting. Rhythms on
the intercom. A scattergun
(a local pub is round the corner).
　Syncopations prevalent
in times of peace replaced by war
and all the marching feet and meter.
　Poets and their advocates
inside a makeshift ambulance.
The songs to sing are similar –
the crooning in-between the spaces.
　Flurries of activity,
an urban past a distant myth,
a life in metamorphosis
and life and death a light that casts.

707.
"I will go to Kyiv, and if I do not regain my strength there, it will be easier for me to at least leave this world."

708.
We all move on but certain parties carry on.

709.
Manipulations (call them that)
without restrictions
   wander off in obsolescence.

710.
   Syllables amending, twisting
   memories of what's been said
and what's forgotten.

711.
   Gangs in search of would-be sailors
   on a voyage of inspiration,
   desperation on the way.

712.
Away with idiosyncrasy, with its self-indulgent
obsessions and useless posturing at the side of
the road while society moves on regardless.

713.
   Faustus played here once
but now his ghost has gone,
replaced by fashion off-the-peg.

714.
Ideas meet, converse and argue.

715.
>When observed, they never flow.

716.
Transformed from what they should be doing
   into something fascinating.

717.
>*Preface* – not a foot awry
unless of course it's awkward prose
where feet and meter matter less
than sprinting fast.

718.
   Rushing headlong for the abyss as time speeds up and the clock approaches its floppy watch state.

719.
   Rhythm is a metaphor for time,
in four-four-time is time in time,
is time encapsulated.

720.
   Flights from dull formality
(or more, familiarity),
exchanging time for fame and immortality
(at least the possibility).

721.
Trochaic lines are all indented.

722.
　Ovid's *Metamorphoses*
in miniature without the myths.

723.
Obscure demeanours, hidden depths,
remembered lines and perfect timing.

724.
　Subject matter saying you're no good for others
　who reply you're not so good yourself you bastard.

725.
　Subjects to pontificate
about without integrity
(the contrast undeniable).

726.
A *Metamorphoses* of sorts.

727.
The health and safety course be damned.

728.
Obscure demeanours, hidden depths,
forgotten lines and dreadful timing.

729.
　Comments made while in a state of mild inebriation have offended others,
　who, in need of succour, feel aggrieved, and fail to flower due to my ill wind.

730.
Plurality of purpose seeks democracy of thought.

ILLUSTRATION 1010

801-830. Preface Afterword Entries *826* and *827* also from Rarot, *Literary Pictures of Kyiv* 2022.

801.
Ovid Covid Covid Ovid. Ovid
without Covid, Covid without Ovid.
Ovid with or without Covid. Covid
with or without Ovid. Covid killed
a million people in the USA –
statistics from the twelfth of May
two-thousand-twenty-two and who's
to blame for this? Well you-know-who!

802.
A secret floor below the lower basement
 floor and unbeknown to customers.
A door behind the disappointment
 counter (nondescript in nature,
 painted in magnolia)
admits a store detective who
escapes a moment, texting thoughts
about department stores in general.

803.
 Poets and their janissaries
 (in their cups) are fond of feeling.

804.
Contents of a world of paint
(though in the making).

805.
Lower orders utter prose
while upper strata versify in plays
(back in the good old days).

806.
Prose weighed more in the nineteenth century
– the novel to blame for that.

807.
Perhaps we'll act as characters.

808.
You want a verse to run?
Then give its feet a decent pair of
  trainers.

809.
  Buy them, slowly wear them down.

810.
The soles have nothing left to give.

811.
Bombarding page or screen with waves
of interference.

812.
In musical duets performance
   often outshines lyrics (Doris
   Day and Howard Keel a case
in point, their *I Can Do Without You*
   one of many fine examples).

813.
   Who grows restless? Let them fight.
And who grows lazy? Let them write.

814.
A Sunday roast.

815.
It's in the verse (you might have noticed).

816.
   When do parts or particles
a part of something else become
just parts or particles again**?**

817.
Like snookers to be conquered with a cue.

818.
And when the parts or particles
become a wave do parts apart
become a part of something else –
an undertow or undercurrent?

819.
   Content (not content, for sure)

820.
The parts were modified to match
the pairs they were compared against.

821.
A chance to change the argument.

822.
The gamut of it from the backing
   beat to debris on the concert floor.

823.
To call a poet arrogant is arrogant.

824.
Economy and composition.

825.
   Exclamation, extramural,
   ex cathedra extra time extravaganza.

826.
   Random tests were made throughout the process but the ones in *203* became a template.

827.
"As soon as we go underground, we satisfy the need to participate in the life of this city, and the exit from the metro becomes the same as the ritual of cleansing."

828.

"And even lower and to the left, stretching towards the Oboloñskie meadows, the Paddle roars and chatters, always worried about something, poor and enterprising, combining the southern coastal turmoil with the dignity of an average place, full of antiquities and silence."

829.

Entries here are free and equal,
not beholden to another.

830.
Middle of the road
(you'll get run over)

ILLUSTRATION 1011

901-930. Preface Appendix

901.
 Football team and substitute.

902.
Conversing with each other over distances of time and space.

903.
Manipulated during this accumulation (call it that).

904.
Transformed perhaps.

905.
Or maybe not.

906.
Pronounced clavé in most online discussions of the Bo Diddley beat and its histories, especially by American commentators.

907.
A mix of poetry and prose with both exchanging traditional duties.

908.
   Preface as a metaphor
for verse (the explanation's worse).

909.
Occasional anomalies
allowed but only on a whim,
to keep the population guessing.

910.
   Conversations carry on,
self-moderating, self-policing exercises.

911.
   Poems disagree, like you and me,
on many points, and quarrel often.
   Mostly though, they sit together,
   happy in diverse opinions –
   no-one getting hurt at least.

912.
The meter's thesis,
   all the rest antithesis,
and this of course a synthesis.

913.
The greatest passions born in structures
   seen as insupportable by some.

914.
As drawings, not as paintings.

915.
   Verses have intelligence.

916.
Proximity of verse transforms,
proximity of prose transforms,
proximity of quotes transforms,
proximity of poetry,
proximity of doggerel,
proximity of photographs,
proximity of notes transforms.

917.
The utopian quality of fine rather than applied arts (where radical or revolutionary change has less of an impact on everyday life) allows for freedom of thought and assumption.

918.
The concierge is fast asleep.

919.
How could you, Cupid, rape my verse?
I am the Muses' voice, not yours.

920.
I'm dull. I'm sorry, I'm more dull
than you. Excuse me, I'm the dullest.
   Sorry, darling, we're all dull.
I disagree, I'm feeling better
   (it's the weather). Really! Look,
this extra line has done the trick.
Indeed? The work I've gone through just
to get this far! Why did you bother?
   Meanwhile, sunshine over there
is perfect. Is there any justice?

921.
   Rhythm sitting side by side with naturalism.

922.
   Ovid Diddley

923.
   -isms merely constructs in disguise.

924.
The perfect fit for what's been wanting.

925.
   Entries are all spoken for.

926.
A list of famous movie quotes in meter –
   Mrs. Robinson, you're trying to seduce me. Aren't you?
   Is it safe?
You ain't heard nothin' yet!
Forget it, Jake, it's Chinatown.
The greatest trick the devil ever pulled.
I love the smell of napalm in the morning.
   After all, tomorrow is another day!
The stuff that dreams are made of.
   Soylent Green is people!
   Why so serious?
They call me Mister Tibbs!
They call it a Royale with cheese.
To boldly go…
You're gonna need a bigger boat.
Your mother was a hamster and your father smells of
        elderberries!
   I'm not drinking any fucking Merlot!
   Not my tempo.
   I'm the guy who does his job.
Get off my lawn.
I want to be alone.
Good morning, Vietnam!
They'll never take our freedom!
   May the Force be with you.
   I'll have what she's having.
   I'll be back.
I feel the need—the need for speed!
It's gonna be a bumpy night!
The Dude abides.
You had me at "hello".

926b.

The films – *The Graduate, Marathon Man, The Jazz Singer, Chinatown, The Usual Suspects, Apocalypse Now, Gone with the Wind, The Maltese Falcon, Soylent Green, The Dark Knight, In the Heat of the Night, Pulp Fiction, Star Trek, Jaws, Monty Python and the Holy Grail, Sideways, Whiplash, The Departed, Gran Torino, Grand Hotel, Good Morning, Vietnam, Braveheart, Star Wars, When Harry Met Sally, The Terminator, Top Gun, All About Eve, The Big Lebowski, Jerry McGuire.*

927.
   Try them, try them on again.

928.
A fluid draining from a glass.

929.
Excruciating exegesis.

930.
   Apples are a world of paint in abstract art.

About the author

Rushton has had three books published by erbacce-press prior to *Preface Metamorphoses* (*Burning a Paper Plate…*of 2015, *towards a new art* of the same year, and *lines written…while considering Ovid in translation* from 2019).

He started writing verse in 2004 to complement his art practice, performing on radio (Resonance FM) and in London's East End. From 2015 to 2017 he co-ordinated *poetryartexchange (Romania/UK)*, an international collaborative project involving exhibitions, gigs and an online book of the same name. Between 2018 and 2020 he received an Arts Council England grant for *Constanta Project*, a poetry and art collaboration based in Romania involving conferences, exhibitions, gigs (with his band *Ovid with Reverb*) and an online book *Notes (on comparing English Translations by Christopher Marlowe and John Dryden from Ovid's Amores 1.1, 1.4 & 2.19)*, a mix of poetry, art and research published by Contemporary Literature Press. *Various Wanted* was published by Timpul in 2021, a collaboration with MARGENTO and Taner Murat that continues the Ovid theme. He is also a drummer, illustrator and translator (for Literary Waves Publishing) and co-organises VENT, an international spoken and written word programme, part of Ventnor Fringe Festival. He lives on the Isle of Wight.